Finance Tips & Tricks for Divorcees

AUSTRALIAN EDITION

VOLUME 1

First published in 2022

Copyright © Richard Zados and Daniel Donnelly

Sherwood Finance Limited
4/129 Kensington High Street
London W8 6BD England

The moral rights of the authors have been asserted.

ISBN: 978-0-6454035-4-1 (pbk)

The right of Richard Zados and Daniel Donnelly to be identified as the authors of this work has been asserted by them in accordance with the *Copyright Amendment (Moral Rights) Act 2000*.

All rights reserved. Except as permitted under the Australian *Copyright Act 1968*, no part of this publication may be reproduced, stored in a retrieval system, or transmitted in any form or by any means, electronic, mechanical, photocopying, recording or otherwise without prior written permission from the author.

Contents

1.	Preparation	3
2.	Finding the right lawyer	9
3.	Lawyer checklist.	15
4.	Businesses Concerns	24
5.	Lending criteria	29
6.	Lender checklist	33
7.	Division of the Property	40
8.	Auction or Private treaty	43
9.	Banker or Finance Broker	55
10.	Glossary of Terms	64

Introduction

This handbook will serve as a guide to help in the divorce process and the financial hurdles you may face. This means that you must be involved to make sure you reach the ideal outcome.

You might need a lawyer and financial advice to help you through the divorce process. Individuals hope lawyers protect them from family law dispute, but that's not always the case. You owe it to yourself and to any children you may have to hire the ideal lawyer.

The complications of decoupling can be more challenging than you may think. Before removing a person from a mortgage, the lender will assess the financial circumstances to see if they can support the entire outstanding mortgage on their own.

We hope this book will help you with your expectations when dealing with the legal fraternity and financial process. In doing so, you will avoid costly mistakes and make sure a satisfactory outcome.

1 Preparation

As it can be stressful, you may make wrong decisions. Most cases live with consequences, and on completion you may not change a divorce settlement. If you can alter something, the cost of doing so could be large.

Because of the litigation and emotional grief, you experience at such a time, you may even be at risk of losing your job since you cannot give your work the attention it needs. As a parent, you may be less able to give your children the emotional support they need, not to be underestimated by any means.

Make a list of your immediate and future expectations and any issues you may believe could compromise your objectives and discuss these with your lawyer.

> You should not ignore the necessity of having a safe and peaceful place to stay and collect your thoughts. This may mean getting an order preventing your spouse from entering your home. Whether you prefer to go to a shelter, live with family, rent an apartment, or, if possible, buy a new home.

Setting your expectations

Consider the following factors when deciding the ideal outcome.

- Home and family life
- Finances and career opportunities
- Living an ethical and spiritual life
- Physical state and health
- Social and cultural activities
- Psychological well being

Organise Your Thoughts

Your expectations must not include unrealistic wants; These will ruin the work you've put into it. Be sure to drop contradictory ideas from your thinking as you outline each of your expectations.

Setting your expectations

Before you hire a lawyer make decisions that will affect your life and your family and document these. This chapter will help you prepare your thinking and put things into place. Gather all the information you need to make sure that you are well prepared.

You can create the roadmap for your plans by writing down your goals and objectives. Rather than leaving behind what you have done so far, work toward achieving what you want for the future.

As circumstances and needs change, you may decide to revise your list. Do not consider changing or getting rid of specific goals. Instead, you could think of modification as a victory in that you had the insight to realise a change was necessary and the energy to be proactive.

It is helpful to organise your plans and objectives once you have identified them. Although the order of your goals will depend on what you decide, you should at the very least separate them between those you feel are urgent and those you think are long term.

When you have identified your goals, specify the actions you will need to take to meet them and assign a reasonable timeframe. When setting your goals, consider the following immediate and long-term issues:

- Is there any aspect that requires more attention?
- For example, when can I buy a house?

- Are there any issues related to co-parenting?

- Are you willing to let your children live with your ex-partner, or do you prefer they live with you?

- If your ex-partner has access to your children, how much contact do you like them to have?

- Both parents should try to act positively towards their children.

- List your concerns and the steps you must take.

With children, long-term issues are often not different from immediate ones. These are some of the problems that need to be considered in the long term.

- Education (Private or public? Which school?)

- Religion as upbringing

- Health concerns last a long time.

- Contact during school holidays and special occasions such as Christmas and birthdays

A liable parent must pay child support based on the incomes of the paying and receiving parent. For further information, please visit the Child Support Agency's website at www.csa.gov.au.

A divorce will have lasting effects on both parties. For

1   Preparation

example, financial circumstances will change. Assets could be frozen, and liabilities may double (e.g., child support payments, added household expenses, and spousal maintenance orders).

You should research what you can expect during the divorce process. Visit www.familycourt.gov.au. This informative tool will help you understand the entire divorce process, as it provides step-by-step guides to proceedings in the Family Court.

Perhaps you have sought marriage counselling or individual therapy to save your relationship. but, even if you end up divorcing and none of those strategies work, you must recognise how significant the decision is.

Unfortunately, certain events will occur as soon as you or your spouse decide to move forward. This is a stressful phase. To make sure you emerge from this process in the best shape possible, you need to focus on what you are doing, how you prioritise your activities and what goals you set for yourself in the immediate future and onwards.

It is understandable that when you decide; you feel that the best thing to do is to have a dramatic change and start with a clean slate. But be cautious. Do not make any drastic changes. Do not take on too much at one time. Instead, do things in manageable chunks by organising your time. Set aside a period each day for relaxing activities. Attend to your children's needs and your own.

It is wise to view the process as a negotiation, and if you cannot compromise and agree with your spouse, you might need to hire a lawyer.

2 Finding the right lawyer

There are many lawyers out there that could be the perfect fit for you. For example, suppose a large percentage of their caseload involves Family Law. Better yet, find a law firm that specialises only in family law. In that case, a niche expert will be better for your case rather than hiring someone whose skills span a range of practices.

Remember, its essential to find a family lawyer within your state with local knowledge. So, look out for advertisements in your area, ask around for recommendations and check state law societies to do the worthwhile research before hiring.

Your lawyer will recommend many things, but you are the one who must make the last call. There is an inherent contradiction in the Family Court system. For divorce cases to flow, the court relies on lawyers, but those lawyers are often spending the assets of the very people they are trying to protect.

Whether your lawyer takes control or reacts, the legal fees will stay the same, so be sure to encourage them to be proactive. The case will become intractable if neither spouse's lawyer takes control, resulting in astronomical fees for professionals who follow procedure, but neglect to look after their clients' interests.

You will experience emotional issues but dealing with these with your lawyer can change the focus of your case. Be aware that in bringing these up, your lawyer may decide to draw you into expensive litigation instead of helping to arrange the more critical aspects of your case and providing you with a secure financial future. In other words, try not to be emotional with your lawyer and focus on the practical issues at hand.

Depending on your expectations, no matter who you hire complications will arise. But it will save you hours of legal expenses if you are prepared before meeting the lawyer. Be sure to give information about yourself and your spouse, including full names, dates and places of birth, citizenship, and residential addresses.

An experienced family lawyer is a good negotiator because aggressiveness can be costly, and no one will win. During their lifetime many people will experience divorce. Finding and working with a lawyer you do not know is hard enough, without dealing with the pain of divorce. You can start your search by asking relatives, friends, or acquaintances who went through a divorce if they can recommend a friendly and practical person. You should consider their recommendation seriously.

2 Finding the right lawyer

But do not assume that the lawyer they referred will suit your circumstances.

> Both parties need to realise that divorce is the worst investment they have ever made. You cannot borrow money against it, but you can go broke because of it. When finding the best lawyer, you may feel as if you are searching for a hero in the great legal ocean. But, if you can choose from a wide range of candidates, you are more likely to make the right decision.

It may be worthwhile to ask questions and compile necessary information before deciding who to hire. Ask the person recommending:

- How responsive were they answering your emails and phone calls?
- Were your questions correctly answered
- As they went through each step of the process, did their lawyer explain how everything worked and the outcomes and consequences?
- The lawyers' fees and costs
- Did the lawyer estimate the overall cost of the case?
- Were their estimates correct

- What was their opinion of the amount charged and why?

- Were they satisfied with their lawyer's aggressiveness?

- How well prepared and organised was their lawyer?

- Was their lawyer prepared in advance for essential matters, such as filing documents and hearings, or were these things left until the last minute and handled in a crisis environment?

- What did they think of the way their lawyer handled their case? Did it meet their expectations?

- Was there an action plan in place?

- Did their lawyer have too many other matters giving their case the attention it deserved?

- Is this lawyer someone they would use again? What would prevent them from doing so?

A lawyer who advertises may offer you excellent service if your situation is straightforward. Those who promote might have a 'volume' practice meaning that most of their cases are likely to be easy to close. A lawyer with a high volume of cases is less likely to give you personalised, detail-oriented service. However, one with such a high volume may charge a lower fee. Just remember to do the much-needed research to get the best possible outcome.

To understand how divorce proceedings work and how attorneys work in a Family Court setting, there is nothing quite like seeing how it works. Attend a hearing at the court to see the players in action and experience the atmosphere. Public access to the Courthouse is available.

Spectators can see how a lawyer interacts with their client before and during a hearing. You may choose the right lawyer by observing their behaviour before you hire them. So, see how a courtroom works and how lawyers conduct themselves. Attend the hearings and trials during the weeks leading up to your proceedings.

Lawyers can consume a percentage of the family's assets through excessive fees; the best outcome is for both parties to work together and compromise without lawyers. Consider the children's living arrangement and how much time they will spend with each parent. Secondly, how are the financial assets going to be divided? We provide more information in a later topic.

> If you cannot negotiate and reach a compromise, consider engaging a professional mediator instead of a lawyer. Although assuming you move ahead and are satisfied with your lawyer's projected services, you will need the following information and documents. Remember to send these materials to your lawyer as soon as possible after you hire them.

3 Lawyer checklist.

Gather the documents and records about your real estate assets. Collect copies of documents not only for the registered titles in your name but for all the properties for which you or your spouse are responsible. In addition, any ownership interests may have, or property owned by either name, jointly with another person, or by a trust or business in which you each have a claim.

Establishing and documenting your property ownership history is crucial. It is typical for the person who inherits the property in a divorce to take on tax implications of the sale of the real estate. When you know the history of the land's use, you can analyse any financial or environmental risks of owning the property.

Keep a record of all the properties you have owned, including those you have sold. Make sure you have any supporting documentation. Make sure that the history table is the first document in your real estate file. Organise the supporting documents and attach them to the file folder. You will need:

- Address, price, and date purchased
- Amount of deposit payment and source of funds

- Amount and balance of the original loan
- If they have repaid the mortgage, the date of discharge
- Your list of improvements and their cost
- Insurance proceeds received from claims
- Repair costs for any damage or restoration
- Date of sale, sale price, costs of sale, net profits and how net proceeds were used

You can avoid or plan for problems associated with your real estate. The family home is the most accessible asset to describe, at least on the surface. You should consider how you want to own your home and other properties. Other things to consider include:

- Which property do you believe is yours and should not be divided by the court?
- What property does your spouse own that the court should not divide?
- Would you consider selling the family home?
- Are you willing and able to keep your home and buy out your soon-to-be ex-spouse,
- Are you will accept a pay-out figure from ex-spouse

3 Lawyer checklist.

Motor Vehicles/Boats

For each vehicle or boat either own, list the make, model, fair market value, and debt amount. In addition, give details of the registered owner (s).

Bank Accounts

Include the name of the institution, the names of the account holders, and the balances.

Securities

If you or your spouse own any investment accounts such as stocks, bonds, certificates of deposit and mutual funds give the broker's name, and a description of the assets.

Future Interests

List interests either you or your spouse have in stock options, options to buy stock, unfunded deferred compensation plans, or future ownership rights that might or might not be vested or valued.

Other Assets

You and your spouse should list other assets they own. Examples are:

- Partnering, trusting, collecting, antiques

- Include all properties owned before you married, inherited, inherited as a gift, or gained in exchange for any of the properties described before

- Are there properties owned before the marriage, inherited, received as a gift, or gained as an exchange for any already described properties?

Liabilities

Together, you and your spouse should list debts you are both responsible for paying. Include the balance due, the monthly payment, and any properties used as collateral. Next, make a list of debts you alone pay. You should list the balance due, the monthly payment, and any collateral for the loan.

Both you and your spouse should list credit cards you hold. Name each credit card, including the credit limit. If you carry a balance, the balance owed and the monthly payment, the primary cardholder and any allowed users.

Have you or your spouse borrowed money from family or friends? If so, offer details of the loan, the balance owed and repayment terms.

Expenses

Make a list of your fixed expenses. For instance, medical care, mortgage payments, education, utilities, and other loans. Then show the costs that vary each month. Examples include groceries, recreation, entertainment, and holidays.

Income Tax

Has the Australian tax office sent you or your spouse a letter or tax assessment on prior year's return? If so, please describe its contents. How did you and your spouse file your tax returns during your marriage, joint or separate? Do you or your spouse have a tax debt? If so, for how many years and the balance owing?

Bankruptcy

Do you or your spouse have a bankruptcy pending?

Employment

- Provide your employers contact details
- How long they have employed you for
- Your title or occupation
- Pay frequency (give a copy of your most recent pay statement)
- Any added income you may receive from employment (including what and how often you receive it)
- Self-employment (if not employed)
- Net income before taxes for the past five years
- Any benefits received and any related out-of-pocket expenses
- All the above concerning your spouse

Details of the marriage

- Marriage date and location
- Copy of marriage certificate
- Physical separation date (physical separation being living in separate households)

- Living and sleeping arrangements if you and your spouse have not yet separated but are living under the same roof

- Any earlier separations

- Any prior marriages

- Are there any existing other orders or proceedings with family law?

- Who filed for a divorce or family law proceeding in this marriage (include the file numbers)

- Was the application denied or granted? if it granted the application, include copies of any court orders you received

Children

- Children born during this relationship/marriage

- List each child's full name, date of birth and place of birth

- Where do your children go to school? What kind of school is it: a public school, a private school, or a special school? Describe for each child name of their school, grade, and cost of school fees/day-care fees.

- Enrolment should your children attend a school other than a public school

- Prices of your children's education to be paid.

- if any children's special educational needs, and how they were met in the past and what they will need

- Children from an earlier relationship or marriage

- Child support to/from your former spouse (including the amount of support paid/received per month)

- Receipt of child support, details of payments required, as well as any back-payments owed.

- Any residency arrangements and contact information in place

- Any current contracts for residency and contact

- In determining spousal maintenance, your net disposable income is considered, as well as your child support obligation.

Special Needs

- If you, your spouse, or your children suffer from a physical, mental, or psychiatric illness or disability or need health care, home care, accommodation, or education. Describe the condition and when diagnosed.

3   Lawyer checklist.

- The details of your spouse, child, or you are under the care of a doctor, counsellor, or psychologist.

- The details of your spouse, child, or you take any medication.

- Details of your spouse, your child, or any other treatment

- Costs of any medication or treatment (after payment by insurance)

4 Businesses Concerns

If you are a business operator, divorce can affect its operations. Business partnerships between divorced couples present several issues. The Family Court has the authority to issue orders affecting business assets against third parties (business partners). As a result, the court orders could affect business partners, family trusts, and even banks. For example, the Family Court may make an order advising the bank that, even if both parties are jointly liable for a mortgage, they can only pursue one party for the balance owing on the mortgage.

There are many business records that lawyers, financiers, and accountants will need since both you and your spouse will get divorced. This is because the real value of the business is based on derived income and calculating the asset value.

Lenders, assess public company directors as employees in mortgage applications. In contrast, directors of smaller firms have ownership of shares and are self-employed borrowers. Since shareholders own the company, they can control how much income they receive.

It is common for directors to receive smaller salaries. In addition, directors' income can be less stable than

4 Businesses Concerns

an employee. As a result, it can sometimes be more challenging for company directors to get and sustain a mortgage. Not only that, but when company accounts are constructed to minimise tax (which can be done by showing the least amount of money available for taxation), it does not show the company's real financial position, which can cause the complications.

Determining the salary of a sole trader or a company is challenging for the lender's credit team. Financial institutions will use the company's net profit before tax as a base for assessing how much a client can borrow. Lenders can add back depreciation, superannuation contributions, non-reoccurring interest payments, for servicing the loan on a case-by-case basis.

> A low documentation mortgage could be the answer to overcome this situation because this form of financing does not need the standard financial information mentioned earlier. Several lenders will consider a letter from the client's existing accountant to support the borrower's current income. In addition, they will need that the company or sole trader has been registered with an Australian business number (ABN) for at least two years.

As a business owner, you will need to give your lawyer with the following information about your business interests:

- A share certificate proving ownership of the business
- List of other shareholders and their shareholdings
- The names of the directors and the company secretary
- Amounts owed to investors, partners, or owners
- How ownership was gained in the business may be found in any trust or estate planning documents
- Documents showing current or future ownership structure of trusts or other estate planning documents
- List any loans or debts that you have guaranteed either on your own or with your spouse
- The company must list the benefits it provides to you, your spouse, your children, or other family members, as well as the costs associated with providing those benefits.
- The last three years' income tax returns
- Financial statements for the previous three years

4 Businesses Concerns

- Three years' worth of BAS (Business Activity Statements) statements
- Accounts schedule
- Current receivables
- Accounts payables – current
- An inventory of assets with their location and current market value, not depreciation
- Any recent business valuations
- Purchase, sale, or partnership agreements
- Major customers contributing to your business. List these

Other things to consider:

Discuss the following to make sure the business continues operating during the divorce.

- Both spouses should be involved in day-to-day management of the business.
- Keeping employees comfortable
- There might be questions about the ownership interest and its structure.

- When determining child or spousal maintenance, establishing a correct income figure is of utmost importance.

- The valuation of the business

- The tax implications are transferred from one spouse to another when the business is sold or redeemed shares.

- Buying out the interest of one spouse

- When the business is based at home, moving the operation may be a choice

- Staying connected with other business partners or owners if any

- The cost of legal and accounting services can increase if the divorce process gets out of hand.

5 Lending criteria

Australia has four leading banks, each of which owns several smaller banks regulated by federal government entities (the Australian Securities and Investments Commission and the Reserve Bank of Australia). One of the most recent innovations in mainstream lending is the emergence of non-conforming lenders. The first lenders emerged in the 1990s as competition created a void in the middle market, filling a gap between traditional and private lenders that lend on property, sometimes as a last resort.

To set their mortgage rates, non-confirming lenders use a method known as risk-based pricing. These leaders play a critical role in the Australian lending market because they charge customers an interest rate that reflects their risk of defaulting on their mortgages.

Non-conforming lenders support borrowers who have trouble getting home loans from mainstream lenders. For various reasons, those with a damaged credit history are self-employed or have jobs with irregular income streams, such as consultants and freelancers (for example). They begin with higher interest rates, reducing or refinancing back to standard mortgage terms.

These lenders are ideal for divorce settlements, as its common for joint credit cards and home loan accounts to be managed poorly during divorce settlements. There are subprime lenders that will consider accounts that are in arrears and will fund the account upon settlement. But the loan amounts are limited. Give us call and we can do the research for you.

> If both spouses keep immaculate conduct on outstanding joint liabilities throughout the process, the terms of finance will be sharper, and loan amounts are not limited. But all lenders will need the separation agreement and or court orders before finalising the financial arrangements.

The lender looks at several factors to decide whether you are a reliable and upstanding individual with an excellent reputation and, thus, speaking, a safe prospect.

Your ability to service the loan — lenders examines you to figure whether you can afford to service a particular loan size based on your income and expenses. Their consideration includes how many dependent children you have.

5   Lending criteria

Your assets — Even though your new home is likely to be your biggest asset, a lender will want to know what other assets you have accumulated to understand how your money is being spent. Your assets may include a car, large furniture or home appliances, a share portfolio and a superannuation account.

Lenders, review your credit history — credit reports. The lender will review your credit obligations and whether you have settled your balances on outstanding bills. If you don't keep on top of your financial comings and goings, your credit score and outcome of the credit application could suffer.

Your employment conditions — To qualify for a loan, you need to have been employed by a single employer for at least three months. Unless you have industry experience several lenders will consider the 2income.

As part of the application, you will need to show the details of your liabilities, such as payments, outstanding amounts, and the lender that provided the credit. For example, the lender will want to know the limit and include the total repayment amount in the servicing calculator despite even the smallest balance on your credit card or the payment you make. Sometimes, they may even ask that the account be closed before settlement.

6 Lender checklist

To complete the divorce settlement by refinancing or purchasing a new property, you will need following documentation for most lenders.

- Proof of income
- Pay slips from the past two or three months
- A score of 100 for identification
- Most recent Payment summary
- Tax returns for two years – self-employed applicants
- List of monthly and annual living expenses
- Evidence of any other income, such as rental income or Centrelink payments, should be provided
- The address where you have lived for the past three years
- The last three years' employment history
- When you started working at this company
- The cost of living each month

Disclaimer other documents could be required.

What is equity release?

In terms of mortgages, the word equity is used to describe the difference between what you owe on your home loan and the property's value. Equity release is a widespread practice among lenders. Overall, one of the best ways to reduce lending risk.

Depends on the property's risk profile, a bank may even pay for a third party to value the property instead. The valuer will often describe the house and research what properties with similar attributes have sold. Most banks will have no problem with sharing the valuer's report with the borrowers.

As mentioned earlier, when calculating how much equity a property holds, the amount of debt and the value of a property are the most crucial factors, although it can be reliant on the valuation (which most lenders will need before applying).

> It's always important to remember that valuation companies can be more conservative than others. They often have a different outlook on the property market. They need to consider the price that they believe someone could sell the property for.

Lenders Mortgage Insurance

When the LVR (Loan to Value Ratio) exceeds 80 per cent of the property value, a lender will impose a fee known as lenders mortgage insurance (LMI) as a single payment (which, in most cases, is added to the total loan).

If a borrower defaults on the mortgage and the property sale does not cover the losses, mortgage insurance protects the lender's investments. The insurance covers the difference between the sale price and the remaining mortgage.

> The borrower pays the insurance premiums, but the insurance does not help them, although they may not borrow as much without it. A mortgage insurance contract is made between the insurer and the lender and is not refundable to the borrower. so, even if they buy another property, it cannot be transferred to a new mortgage.

Interest rates

Standard variable

Standard variable rates are often the first interest rates mentioned when speaking with lenders about home loans and their features and benefits. Most banking institutions offer this under a different name. Still, full-service loans can be a good fit for most borrowers, making the lending decision smoother and quicker for those with no special requirements or issues. when discussing rising or falling mortgage interest rates, media outlets cite this figure, known as the SVR. SVRs are the highest interest rate charged to mortgage customers, but they may include other products, which may be helpful. Offset accounts, redraw accounts and fee-free general banking are notable examples.

Despite being the most often quoted rate, few customers pay it. most banks discount the offered interest rate from the loan to value ratio, especially for property investors who have a higher-than-average loan balance.

Discount variable rates.

Discount variable rates for no-frills mortgages are advertised lower than standard variable rates. but these will not always offer access to products such as offset accounts, redraw accounts and fee-free banking.

With low-value properties, these low ever rate products may be a good choice for starters. Even if you buy a more expensive first property, the Bank may offer you the extra features with a standard rate instead of an interest rate associated with a discounted mortgage.

Fixed or Variable

Choosing between variable and fixed-rate loans is critical. Before buying a home, be sure to weigh each mortgage's advantages and disadvantages.

Each has its pros and cons; the important considerations are whether a fixed or variable rate will be ideal for your needs.

If you want more certainty apply for a fixed rate. A fixed rate will allow you to fit your repayments into your budget without having to worry about any interest fluctuations.

While most lenders have a buffer and review your living expenses before offering finance. When the interest rate increases, the property owners might struggle to meet the requirements of their higher monthly repayments.

> When considering variable rate loans, you may make unlimited contributions to the mortgage. In contrast, fixed-rate repayments are capped per annum, and how much varies with the lender.

The offset Account

An offset account, not available with all loans, may prove to be a valuable extra string in your bow. Offset accounts give the borrower the freedom to deposit and save money, as well if linked to your mortgage loan account, it offsets the interest charged on the balance of the loan amount.

For example, with a mortgage loan balance of $500,000 and $40,000 sitting in the offset account over the month, interest is calculated on a loan balance of $460,00 because of the $40,000 sitting in the offset account. Keep in mind the lender charges interest daily on the balance of the loan account, so money going in and out of the offset account will affect the amount of interest saved.

There is only one offset account with a loan package, so attach the offset account to the home loan mortgage to offset the interest charged. There is no benefit to attach an offset account to an investment property loan, as all the interest charged is tax deductible.

Interest-only loans

When buying a property to occupy you need a good explanation for why you are applying for interest-only loans. Satisfactory reasons do exist, but it is better to speak with us before choosing that lender, as we can suggest a lender that is opened to only offering interest on loans. A downside of interest-only loans is that the balance owed does not decrease with the property's value, so if the property's value drops, you might need to borrow more money to cover the difference or end up with negative equity.

Credit report

Joint mortgages, credit cards or personal loans are listed on your individual credit report. During the divorce process if these are not paid on time, you run the risk of tarnishing your credit file, which could impact your ability to borrow in future. Comprehensive credit reporting assists lenders in making lending decisions. Your credit report will show that by a numerical figure. The higher credit score, the better chance in getting approval. A lower score can either result in higher interest rates or rejection.

7 Division of the Property

The complications of decoupling can be more challenging than you may think. From a finance perspective, all owners must agree to transferring equity, and then the solicitor will have to register it at the land registry. In addition, if the transfer involves removing a joint mortgage holder or adding a new mortgage holder, the lender will need to approve it.

Before removing a person from a mortgage, the lender will assess the financial circumstances of the other to see if they can support the entire outstanding mortgage amount on their own. As part of this, they get references, statements scrutinised, and the credit history checked for details of any unmanageable debt incurred. Although the credit assessment was completed before the mortgage was originated, circumstances might have changed since then. It is possible, for example, that the remaining party was not the primary earner during the original assessment or that their income had changed.

A lender is unlikely to approve a transfer if there is a risk to the security of the mortgage, so divorced couples who are still joint homeowners cannot go ahead with the transfer. In addition, subject to circumstances, applying

7 Division of the Property

for a mortgage on a new property can be difficult because of the existing mortgage.

A transfer may have a clear or hidden purpose. Lenders will examine the reasons behind the approach to find the borrower's motivations. For example, suppose they transferred equity in a divorce. In that case, one person may need other mortgage financing to buy out the other.

Lenders need to know that if a loan is transferred because of a divorce or separation, the remaining borrower may have or might expect to receive maintenance payments. Because these factors will affect the borrower's ability to repay the loan.

In summary, the lender will assess the risk by considering the borrower's ability to repay the loan, and a review of their overall circumstances. The lender will charge an equity transfer fee and require legal advice (conveyancer) before the transfer can proceed.

Family homes can be a very contentious asset before and after a divorce. In other words, the custodial parents may want to keep the home for the children's sake. So, the value is difficult to estimate; it is challenging to convert to cash and bears federal and state taxes.

The option of selling the home at the right time and dividing the net proceeds is critical. This often happens after a divorce. Couples seldom plan household maintenance and upkeep during a divorce. You may make an irrational or poor decision at the time of the divorce because of your family's emotional attachment to their property, especially a family or holiday home.

> If broker or lender asks you to assemble financial records, organise them as best you can. Its highly recommended to cooperate with your spouse as much as possible. In either case, if you intend to sell or buy, we have listed below the process as a guide for Private Treaty or auction across Australia.

8 Auction or Private treaty

There is no doubt that a good auction can be exciting, whether it is in-house or even held on a suburban street. It can become so intense that the bids can sometimes go beyond what was expected due to popular demand. The aim of an auction is simply to create a large, exciting atmosphere for a sale while also providing bidders and sellers with transparency.

If you are considering bidding at an auction, it's essential that you first set yourself a budget (and a firm limit) before consulting your solicitor or accountant. If you have any enquiries, feel free to contact our team.

If an auction does not meet the vendor's expectations and the final bid is declared to be insufficient by the vendor, the property will often be passed on to the highest bidder or will be reverted to a private treaty sale. The same goes for other situations, too, like if there are no genuine bidders.

Typically, if there are several under-bidders, the sale will be passed in, and the highest bidder will have a private conversation about the vendor's reserve level. Agents are likely to tell everyone involved that there is still a chance to take the property for a higher bid, although the first bidder is given the initial right of refusal. If they're not satisfied with the reserve price, the agents can continue negotiations with under-bidders.

In general, deciding between an auction or private treaty often comes down to producing the best results. In some circumstances, auctions can seem like the best solution, where several investors will be prepared to outdo each other to get the property regardless of the extra money they are investing. Typically, any properties passed during the auction process are sold later through a private treaty sale.

In Australia, many homes are sold by private treaties. Vendors (sellers) determine the price at which their properties are marketed for sale under this process. If the buyer is not happy with the price, they begin negotiations by offering a lower one.

Negotiation is a natural part of buying or selling a property by private treaty. To get the highest price, a seller often looks for a private treaty sale to work like a slow-motion auction, i.e., offers come in and move back and forth between the seller and purchaser. Rather than taking place during a one half-hour auction with other bidders in front of the property, this may take place over hours, and sometimes days, weeks, or even months.

8   Auction or Private treaty

A seller's agent receives the offer. When a vendor agrees to a request, they will ask the agent to accept it, and contracts are then written and exchanged. A private treaty can seem less stressful and more straightforward compared to an auction sale or purchase. However, keep in mind that a private treaty does require more negotiation skills from the seller.

Some states require that you make an offer in writing, often by filling out a form and signing it. For example, you can put in a verbal offer in New South Wales, Queensland, Victoria, and the Northern Territory and the ACT (Australian Capital Territory), but these will be taken more seriously if they are in writing.

We suggest following the procedure set out in your state or territory. If the vendor agrees to your offer and any conditions you set, you both sign and exchange the contract document, making the agreement legally binding. However, consider the following explanations as a guide because local governments and buyers often scrutinise the auction process, and the process could change.

Victoria

Auction

At the start of the auction, there is no requirement to register your intent to bid, unless it is a condition imposed by the real estate agency. Only the auctioneer may make a vendor bid, and they must announce a 'vendor bid.' If a co-owner intends to bid, the auctioneer must disclose this at the commencement of the auction Bidders can ask the question during the auction if the property is 'on the market.' Dummy bids are prohibited by law. For mortgagee sales, Deceased estates or Family Law Matters, the property must go to auction; therefore, the agent will not be able to convey offers prior to the auction date.

Private treaty

The Estate Agents Professional Conduct Regulations 2018 state all offers must be communicated unless instructed to the contrary in writing by the vendor. In addition to written submissions, buyers can also make verbal offers. If you want the vendor to take you seriously, submit a completed contract of sale and offer a deposit. After the vendor accepts your request, your offer becomes binding only when you and the vendor exchange contracts, and a deposit (usually 10%) is accounted for.

8   Auction or Private treaty

Tasmania

Auction

Having your finance and deposit ready on the day is essential. Vendors may bid up to the reserve price, and the auctioneer must clearly state vendor bids to potential buyers assembled at the auction. If the offers do not reach the reserve, you may be able to negotiate with the vendor afterwards and settle on a negotiated price. Typically, Contracts of Sale are signed and exchanged on the day. Dummy bidding is prohibited.

Private treaty

To make an offer, buyers should use the law society contract of sale provided by their agent. Alternatively, if you wish, you can ask your attorney or conveyancer to prepare the offer document for you. The agent must pass all offers but may not if the request is below the vendor's stipulated amount. Sellers are not required to disclose known defects with the property. A cooling-off period of three days. However, if both parties choose not to use it, no cooling-off period applies. Once the contract of sale is signed by both parties and exchanged finance proceeds.

New South Wales

Auction

To participate or bid at a residential auction, potential buyers must register by showing identification and will be given a bidder's number. The auctioneer oversees the bidding process. The vendor sets the reserve price before the auction and is entitled to one vendor bid. If the reserve price is not met, the highest bidder is asked to negotiate privately with the sales agent. Unless agreed before the auction, a ten per cent deposit is required at the fall of the hammer. Ensure finances are ready as contracts will be exchanged on the day. Dummy bids are illegal.

Private treaty

Offers can be verbal or in writing. Although making a formal offer, the vendor is more likely to accept. When the vendor accepts your request, a five-day cooling-off period begins. The buyers and sellers are not legally bound until signed contracts are exchanged. Then titles are prepared, loan documentation is returned signed, and settlement can be finalised. This typically takes between 30 to 90 days The buyer is required to pay a deposit. The settlement process can usually be finalised within 30 — 90 days.

8   Auction or Private treaty

Australian Capital Territory

Auction

You must register to bid by providing the real estate agent at the auction with proof of your identity, and a bidder's number will be assigned to you. The agent can make one vendor bid on behalf of the vendor and must be clearly stated as a vendor bid. The highest bidder must exceed the reserve price set before the auction commences. If the reserve is not met, the highest bidder will have an opportunity to negotiate privately with the sales agent. The highest bidder will have to sign contracts and pay the agreed deposit on the day. Finance must be in place to meet settlement under absolute terms, and 'dummy bidding' is prohibited

Private treaty

Agents must notify the vendor of all offers and cannot be made verbally and must be in writing. The advertised price must be similar and close to what the seller will accept. The seller can receive offers from other interested parties until contracts are exchanged. The sales agent will send the contract and offer documentation to the buyer's solicitor upon accepting the offer. Once the buyer and seller have both signed and exchanged the contract, it becomes legally binding. The five-day cooling-off period can only be waived or amended with signed approval from the vendor.

Western Australia

Auction

Auctions are not as common in Western Australia as in other states. The auctioneer starts by detailing the benefits of the property and any relevant information and restrictions on the title. In addition, the required deposit to be paid must be disclosed before commencing. The auctioneer then calls for or announces an opening bid, usually below the reserve price. Offers from vendors are permitted. It must be specified in the auction form whether the seller will be making bids and how many. On the fall of the hammer, the agreed deposit will be paid. Contracts exchanged on the day. Dummy bids are illegal.

Private treaty

If you suggest making an offer, buyers must fill out and sign an offer and acceptance contract (O & A). The agent will prepare either of the two forms, Contract for Sale of Land and General Conditions or the Strata Title, and the agent will present the offer to the vendor. The vendor may either accept or counter the offer by amending the O & A or reject it, and the agent is obligated to inform the purchaser. Once the offer is accepted, the settlement must occur within the agreed timeframe.

Queensland

Auction

Before the auction begins, you must register with the auctioneer. A number paddle is provided. Up until the reserve price, vendor bids can be accepted, provided the auctioneer announces them in the conditions of sale at the beginning of the auction. Auctioneers cannot engage in dummy bidding or take false bids. After the auction, contracts are signed, and a five to ten per cent deposit is paid.

Private treaty

Agents can list prices over the minimum the vendor is willing to accept. However, agents are prohibited from listing below the vendors' minimum price, often considered bait advertising, which is an offence. Verbal offers can be made, and all written offers must be sent to the vendor. When your offer is accepted, the agent must provide you with a contract of sale, accompanied by a warning statement. The purchaser will need to pay a deposit after the five-day cooling-off period. This typically takes between 30 to 90 days for settlement.

South Australia

Auction

You must register by providing your identification to the agent conducting the sale. For someone else to bid on your behalf, you will need to provide proof of your identity plus a signed authorisation letter. A reserve price is usually set, in writing, before the auction. You should be aware that the vendor is entitled to three bids. The vendor bids must not exceed the reserve price. The auctioneer must announce each such bid as a 'vendor bid'. If reported throughout the auction, it indicates. The vendor's reserve price is not reached. If you are the highest bidder and the reserve price is not met, you can negotiate privately. At the fall of the hammer, a pay ten per cent deposit is required if you are the successful bidder. It would be best if you had your finance ready because contracts are exchanged on the day. Dummy bids are not allowed

Private treaty

All offers must be in writing that discloses the seller's name, contact information, the price, the settlement date, and any other conditions. Each submission can include a date by which the offer lapses. Before a vendor accepts an offer, the agent must ensure the vendor has received all written offers. Requests are often subject to building inspection and loan approval or any other conditions by the purchaser or vendor. Both parties must sign a contract of sale before the offer is legally binding. To finalise the settlement, it can take from 30 to 90 days.

Northern Territory

Auction

On the day, the auctioneer will detail the terms and conditions of the auction process and then call for bids on the property. All bidders must register by showing identification. The Auctioneers must not engage in conduct that is fraudulent or misleading. Dummy bids are explicitly prohibited. Before the auction, the vendor will set a 'reserve price', and the property will be passed in unless the bidding reaches that point. An auctioneer will often advise the attendees that the property is 'on the market', indicating it has passed the reserve price and will be sold to the highest bidder. If the reserve is not met, bidders are invited to negotiate to purchase the property with the selling agent. As usual, ensure that finance is ready to meet the agreed settlement date.

Private treaty

An offer on a property should be on a formal contract, although buyers can make verbal offers, and all offers must be sent to the vendor. The vendor is not legally bound to accept your submission until the contract of sale are exchanged. At the time of the exchange, the purchaser is required to pay a deposit. The settlement process can take from 30 – 90 days.

9 Banker or Finance Broker

When you require information on a range of financial products and opportunities, it might be worth getting in touch with a finance broker. A good brokerage will have years of experience and will take the time to crunch numbers and compare different loans and work out which one will be the most suitable for your needs. They can also interact with lenders on your behalf and will even put in the effort to work after hours to assist you.

Over time, the complexity and requirements of the industry have significantly increased, leading most to charge upfront fees. In addition, many lenders will have their criteria for assessing applications, and for the most part, these aren't public knowledge – which can cause some concerns for you when trying to find the right deal. This is where a good finance broker comes in, as they will help to save you a great deal of time by advising when to and when not to apply for a loan.

Consider contacting our team before reaching out to your current lender.

Family court directory

Adelaide

Grenfell Centre, Level 5, 25 Grenfell Street,

Adelaide SA 5001 T (08) 8205 2666 F: (08) 8205 2688 E adelaide@familycourt.gov.au

Darwin

TCG Building Commonwealth Law Courts, 80 Mitchell Street Darwin NT 0800 T (08) 8981 1488, or 1800 679 236

accessible anywhere within the NT) F (08) 8981 6081 E darwin@familycourt.gov.au

Albury

Level 1, 463-467 Kiewa Street Albury, 2640 T (02) 6021 8944 F (02) 6021 8964 E: albury@familycourt.gov.au

Dubbo

Commonwealth Offices, Level 2, Cnr Wingewarra and Macquarie Street,

Dubbo NSW 2830 T (02) 6881 1555 F (02) 6884 2972 E dubbo@familycourt.gov.au

Armidale

Beardy Street Mall, Armidale NSW 2350 Contact the Newcastle Registry for further information T (02) 4926 1255 F (02) 4926 5204 E newcastle@familycourt.gov.au

Hobart

Commonwealth Law Courts, 39-41 Davey Street, Hobart TAS 7000 T (03) 6232 1725 F (03) 6232 1723 66 E hobart@familycourt.gov.au

Ballarat

Child & Family Services Building 115 Lydiard Street North Ballarat VIC 3350 T (03) 5337 3333

Launceston

3rd Floor, ANZ Building Cnr Brisbane and George Street, Launceston TAS 7250 T (03) 6334 2111 F (03) 6334 5059 E: launceston@familycourt.gov.au

Brisbane

Commonwealth Law Courts, Cnr North Quay and Bank Street,

Brisbane QLD 4000 T (07) 3248 2200 F (07) 3236 1534 E brisbane@familycourt.gov.au

Lismore

Level 2, Manchester Unity Building 29-31 Molesworth Street,

Lismore NSW 2480 T (07) 3248 2200 (Brisbane Registry) F (07) 3236 1534 (Brisbane Registry) E lismore@familycourt.gov.au

Cairns

Level 4, Commonwealth Government Centre, 104 Grafton Street,

Cairns Qld 4870 T (07) 4041 2377 or 1800 641 080

F (07) 4031 1109 E cairns@familycourt.gov.au

Mackay

12 Brisbane Street Mackay Qld 4740 T Townsville Registry (07) 4722 9333 or 1800 801 668 F (07) 4772 3262 E townsville@familycourt.gov.au

9   Banker or Finance Broker

Canberra

Cnr Childers Street and University Avenue, Canberra ACT 2601 T (02) 6267 0511 F (02) 6257 1586 E: canberra@familycourt.gov.au

Melbourne

Commonwealth Law Courts, 305 William Street,

Melbourne VIC 3000 T (03) 8600 3777 F (03) 8600 3750 E melbourne@familycourt.gov.au

Coffs Harbour

Level 1, 26 Gordon Street,

Coffs Harbour NSW 2450 T (07) 3248 2200 (Brisbane Registry) F (07) 3236 1534 (Brisbane Registry) E brisbane@familycourt.gov.au

Mount Gambier

Grenfell Centre, Level 5, 25 Grenfell Street, Adelaide SA 5001 T (08) 8205 2666 F (08) 8205 2688 E adelaide@familycourt.gov.au

Dandenong

53-55 Robinson Street, Dandenong VIC 3175 Phone: (03) 9767 6200 Fax: (03) 9767 6286 Email: dandenong@familycourt.gov.au

Newcastle

61 Bolton Street, Newcastle NSW 2302 T (02) 4926 1255 Fax: (02) 4926 5204 E newcastle@familycourt.gov.au

Orange

Commonwealth Law Courts, 1-3 George Street,

Parramatta NSW 2123 T (02) 9893 5555 (02) 9893 5600 E parramatta@familycourt.gov.au

Tamworth

Cnr Marius and Fitzroy Str,

Tamworth NSW 2340 Contact the Newcastle Registry for further information T (02) 4926 1255 F: (02) 4926 5204 E: newcastle@familycourt.gov.au

9   Banker or Finance Broker

Parramatta

Commonwealth Law Courts, 1-3 George Street,

Parramatta NSW 2123 T (02) 9893 5555 F (02) 9893 5600 E parramatta@familycourt.gov.au

Townsville

Level 2, Commonwealth Centre, 143 Walker Street, Townsville Qld 4810 Phone: (07) 4722 9333 or 1800 801 668 Fax: (07) 4772 3262 Email: townsville@familycourt.gov.au

Rockhampton

Level 4, Commonwealth Centre, Cnr Fitzroy and East Street,

Rockhampton Qld 4700 T (07) 4921 2939 F (07) 4922 5784 E rockhampton@familycourt.gov.au

Wollongong

Level 1, 43 Burelli Street,

Wollongong, NSW 2500 PO Box 825 Wollongong East 2520 DX Box: DX 5238 Wollongong T (02) 4253 6200 (02) 4228 4770 E: wollongong@familycourt.gov.au

Sydney

Lionel Bowen Building, 97-99 Goulburn Street,

Sydney NSW 2000 T (02) 9217 7111 F: (02) 9217 7134 Compliance Certificates Email: sydney.caseflow@familycourt.gov.au Email: sydney@familycourt.gov.au

Western Australia

150 Terrace Road (Cnr Victoria Avenue),

Perth WA 6000 T (08) 9224 8222 F (08) 9224 8360 E family.court@justice.wa.gov.au Call Centre (08) 9224 8222

Country Free call 1800 199 228

Law Society Directory

Law Society of the Australian Capital Territory

www.actlawsociety.asn.au

Law Society of New South Wales

www.lawsociety.com.au

Law Society of the Northern Territory

www.lawsocietynt.asn.au

9   Banker or Finance Broker

Queensland Law Society

www.qls.com.au

Law Society of South Australia

www.lawsocietysa.asn.au

Law Society of Tasmania

www.taslawsociety.asn.au

Law Society of Victoria

www.liv.asn.au

Law Society of Western Australia

www.lawsocietywa.asn.au

10 Glossary of Terms

Arrangement fees

When lenders charge for the effort of providing financing to a borrower, this fee can vary from one lender to another.

Auction

An auctioneer conducts a sales process in public.

Auctioneer

A profession that oversees the sale of real estate or other items whereby persons become purchasers by competition in public view, the sale favours the highest bidder.

Australian Bureau of Statistics

A federal statutory agency, the Australian Bureau of Statistics (ABS), collects and analyses statistical data and provides evidence-based advice to federal, state and territory governments.

10 Glossary of Terms

Business activity statements (BAS)

BAS is used to reconciling the tax collected by a business is known as Good and Services Tax (GST), paid to the State government, or annual.

Balance

A statement begins with your last statement's balance, which is the amount you had within your account at the end of the previous report.

Bankruptcy

A legal concept that you would be best to avoid. Also known as Insolvency, this occurs when an individual cannot meet their financial obligations within a reasonable time frame or if their liabilities exceed their assets.

Bid

A method of purchasing real estate at Auction by an offering.

Caveat

A property caveat is a claim to a property as a legal document. Creating a caveat allows both parties to claim their share of interest. Until the caveat is settled, no further transactions can be registered against the title.

Capital Gains Tax

If you sell an asset such as investment property for a profit, you are subject to capital gains tax (CGT). At the end of the fiscal year, they add the capital gain to your income to be taxed..

Cheque

Cheques detail any amount of money that's withdrawn since account holders often write the cheque to pay someone. This includes the number on the cheque and the amount taken out.

Court judgement

If a person cannot repay their creditors, creditors can get a judgment in court.

Commercial tenants

Commercial, industrial, and retail properties are standard in arranging long-term leases. In addition, outgoings are negotiated but passed onto the tenant.

Commitment fee

A fee is added onto a loan to compensate a lender for their commitment to offering to fund.

Company secretary

A secretary responsibility is to circulate agendas and other documents to directors, shareholders, and auditors and record minutes of shareholder and directors' meetings and resolutions.

Contract of sale

An agreement includes the terms and conditions signed, dated and witnessed by all related parties.

Conveyance

When real estate is transferred from one party to another, in real estate, this could be when a seller transfers the ownership of a property to a buyer.

Collateral

Collateral is protection to mitigate the risks involved with lending.

Credit

While this refers to several aspects of lending, most used to describe a contract agreement where an individual receives money and repays the lender by a predetermined date (with an added interest fee).

Credit score

Used by lenders to decide whether to accept funding applications based on the risk associated with the borrower. Also referred to as a credit rating.

Development Approval

Local town planning authorities provide written approval of a project, prepared by the developer's or landowner's consultants, allowing the project to move forward as per the development plan.

Deposit

The amount of money needed to be paid upfront as part of the loan agreement. The amount specified can often vary depending on a variety of circumstances.

Division of Property

Fair distribution, or property division, divides property rights and obligations between divorced or De facto spouses and business partners.

Director

An individual manages a company's operations, with the ability to exercise the business' powers for whatever needs it may have.

Economy

A summary of goods, services produced, distributed and sold within a region or country.

Equity

Property equity is the difference between the remaining debt and the asset's capital value in question.

Exchange of Contracts

When a seller and purchased sign a copy of the sale contract and then exchanges these documents creates a binding agreement for the sale of real estate on agreed terms. The parties are then bound to go ahead to settlement, subject to any cooling-off period that may apply.

First mortgage

When a borrower uses the property as security for the first time as collateral for a loan, as usual, if the mortgage repayments are not met as agreed, the lender can seize the security.

Financial position

An organisation's financial position refers to its assets, liabilities, and equity balances. In a broader sense, the concept can describe the financial condition, which is determined by analysing and comparing its financial statements.

GSA (General Security Agreement)

They register GSA on a National Register to secure the lender's interest against the relevant security entity/asset. As part of the Register, lenders can also negotiate a priority system to make sure that their interests are protected and prioritised.

Guarantor

In property development transactions, lenders could need more security to reduce their risk should the developer default on a loan. This guarantee can take various forms, from cash to property.

Gross Realised Value

In property construction, the Gross Realisation Value is the gross sales (or GST exclusive value of the property) upon the completion of the project. Also known as GRV.

Initial Public Offering

When a company raises capital from public investors by offering shares of a corporation in a public share issuance, often abbreviated to IPO.

Interest rate

The amount of interest charged on a loan, in proportion to the amount borrowed, allows a bank or lender to profit when distributing funds.

Investment property

A real estate purchase intends to earn rental income or capital gain.

Indicative offer

Lenders often show or suggest that the offer may proceed if conditions are met, also known as a conditional offer.

Joint and severally

Where all parties are accountable for the full terms of the agreement, they have entered. For example, in a personal liability case, each party will pursue to repay the entire amount owed.

Land tax

Whether you own or an investment property, you will pay land tax. The amounts vary from state to state.

Lawyer

A lawyer is someone who practices law and deals with legal issues. A lawyer provides legal advice and represents people in court.

Land Banking

Refers to financing secured for the acquisition and holding of developmental sites with no certainty of rapid development.

Legal fees

Upon completing the purchase, the solicitor or conveyancer will charge a fee for the legal work carried out during the purchase process. solicitors charge a flat fee regardless of the property's value.

Letter of Offer

When a lender issues a finance offer to a borrower, it can be accepted or rejected depending on the borrower in question acceptance.

Lease agreements

Lease agreements are made between the property owner and tenant to occupy real estate.

10   Glossary of Terms

Loan to Value Ratio

All lenders use a Loan to Value Ratio to assess risk when they consider funding and can have a tremendous impact on the terms offered, abbreviated to LTV (loan to values) or LVR (Loan to Value Ratio).

Litigation

When disputes are resolved in court through litigation, unless the parties settle before trial, a judge may make the final decision for the parties in litigation.

Liabilities

Liabilities are obligations between two parties that have not yet been completed or repaid.

Mortgage

A debt passed onto a borrower from a lender secured by a property.

Mortgagee sale

In the event of a default by the mortgagor, the mortgagee claims the security and resells to avoid economic losses.

Mortgagor

A borrower (individual or company) has an interest in a property through a mortgage as security for credit advancement.

Net Realised Value

The asset value realised on the sale is reduced because of standard deductions. so, often abbreviated to NRV.

Non-conforming loans

The term non-conforming loan refers to lending that does not meet the criteria for bank financing.

Non-recourse loan

When a lender can seize the security if a borrower defaults on their payments, the difference from standard scenarios is that the lender cannot get further compensation, even if the collateral covers the total unpaid loan.

Offshore

Ideal for overseas investors, most offshore financing options are available for competitive prices and offer enticing sums of money. The applications to be considered are company borrowers.

Passed in

If the owner's reserve price has not been met, a property is not sold at Auction; therefore, passed in.

Periodic lease

Typical with residential, a tenant continues to rent and occupy the property beyond the expiration of the lease agreement.

Private treaty sale

The terms and conditions of a private sale between a seller and buyer to purchase the real estate vary from state to state.

Presales

A lender will want a certain number of presales to reduce their risks. While the percentage of resold units is not set, funding can vary from one lender to another.

Principal and interest mortgage

A standard mortgage, with the difference that repayments are part capital and part interest.

Property Acquisition

When legal ownership or rights over real estate are transferred, the rules may vary from one state to another.

Property Maintenance

Property owners will need to decide about building works and maintenance. The agent managing your property will manage and looking after the property. This includes marketing your property, collecting rent and fixing any issues.

Progress Payments

As the construction progresses, Lender's drawdown payments in stages. so, the lender needs to report the work completed by its Quantity Surveyor to compare the completed work as part of the loan agreement.

Property Settlement

A legal process facilitated by the legal and financial representatives of the purchaser and the seller. Settlement occurs when ownership is passed from the seller to the buyer. the settlement date is determined in the contract of sale by the vendor.

Profit

When the financial earnings of a business activity exceed the amount needed for the costs, taxes, etc., this could be when a company buys something and sells it for a higher price.

Preferred equity

Investments or loans exceeding the level associated with project and mezzanine debt but not taking part as equal ranking equity are deemed preferred equity.

Rescind

To discontinue a contract of sale.

Reserve Price

The vendor agrees upon the minimum acceptable price before the Auction.

Residential tenants

In most cases, residential leases last for one year; any shorter would be costly for the property owner for re-tenanting costs such as marketing, rental income delays and re-letting fees to the agent.

Recourse

If the debt obligation is not honoured, a lender may seek a borrower's security. A full recourse is when a lender can take more assets to repay the entire unpaid debt.

Receipt

A note any money that is deposited into your account. This is also known as paid-in or credits.

Reserve Bank of Australia

The Australian central bank publishes and controls monetary policy. This can have a varying, underlying effect on mortgage rates.

Settlement Date

The last part of the process is whereby the purchaser completes the payment of the contract price to the seller, and legal possession is transferred to the purchaser.

Share certificates

A share certificate is a document that is issued by a company that sells shares. An investor receives a share certificate upon purchasing a certain number of shares and as a record of ownership.

Stamp duty

All Australian States and Territories impose stamp duty. The amount varies from state to state. Taxes on business purchases differ from taxes on real estate. It arises from the sale or transfer of a wide range of personal and business assets.

Joint tenants

Joint tenancy is the default type of shared ownership. There is no property division between the joint owners; each owns one hundred per cent of the property. Legal ownership of the property passes to the surviving joint owner when a joint owner dies.

Statement of Position

According to their assets and liabilities, companies or individual positions show the current net equity position.

Security

Security on a mortgage is essential because it reduces the risk a lender takes on when providing a loan. Suppose a loan is backed by property, for example. Then, if the borrower defaults on repayments, the lender may seize the property to claim the outstanding debt.

Share certificates

Whenever a company sells shares on the market, it issues shares certificates. As proof of ownership and as a record of the purchase, shares certificates are issued to shareholders.

Shareholders

A person or business that owns a share in a company's stock. They can receive capital gains, take capital losses, and they may receive dividend payments. They are equity owners and have the same benefits and drawbacks as Directors.

Second mortgage

A borrower can offer their real estate as collateral a second time to another lender while the first still has finance secured. As a result, the subsequent lender takes a second charge over the property.

Senior Debt

The registered mortgage holds the property's first ranking for a primary mortgage or principal debt. Developers often prefer senior debt as the margins are lower since banks or significant mortgage funds provide senior debt.

Tax returns

Tax authorities use this process to assess a taxpayer's liability based on their annual income personal circumstances and includes corporate entities.

Tenants in common

A joint ownership arrangement exists when more than one individual owns the same property, but neither has the right of one hundred per cent ownership of the property.

Valuer

A company appointed to conduct the assessment of the current market value of the real estate.

Variation

To change or alter the conditions of the contract of sale.

Valuation

Not to be confused with an appraisal, as a valuation provides a more accurate and recognised property value.

Vendor

In a real estate transaction, a person (s) or entity sells the property.

Quantity Surveyor

A qualified individual that examines costs associated with the building costs. Market conditions impact labour costs and material suppliers with the DA (development approval). Lenders also engage them to make sure that the project is correctly costed.

Yield

An indicator of income by percentage earnt on real estate. It is Calculated by the received net income and the market value of the real estate.

Zoning

The local council planning controls current and future development, including residential, business, and industrial uses.

For further information about Sherwood Finance:

Call us 1800 743 796

head to the website
www.sherwoodfinance.com.au

follow us on Facebook, Instagram and Twitter.

www.ingramcontent.com/pod-product-compliance
Lightning Source LLC
Chambersburg PA
CBHW030303010526
44107CB00053B/1796